Child Labor

Clive Gifford

A+
Smart Apple Media

TITLES IN THE VOICES SERIES:

AIDS • CHILD LABOR • DRUGS ON THE STREET • GANGS •

HUNGER • POVERTY • RACISM • RELIGIOUS EXTREMISM •

VIOLENCE • VIOLENCE ON THE SCREEN • WAR

Smart Apple Media
P.O. Box 3263, Mankato, Minnesota 56002

U.S. publication copyright © 2010 Smart Apple Media.
International copyright reserved in all countries. No part
of this book may be reproduced in any form without
written permission from the publisher.

This book has been published in cooperation with Evans
Publishing Group.

Copyright © 2009 Evans Brothers Ltd

Printed in China

Library of Congress Cataloging-in-Publication Data
Gifford, Clive.
  Child labor / by Clive Gifford.
     p. cm. -- (Voices)
  Includes index.
  ISBN 978-1-59920-279-2 (hardcover)
  1. Child labor--Juvenile literature. I. Title.
  HD6231.G54 2010
  331.3'1--dc22
                              2008050429

Editor: Susie Brooks
Designer: Mayer Media Ltd
Picture research: Lynda Lines
Graphs and charts: Martin Darlison, Encompass
Graphics

Picture acknowledgements
Photographs were kindly supplied by the following: Alamy
21 (Picture Contact); Associated Press/PA Photos 31, 32;
Corbis 16 (JP Laffont/Sygma), 17 (Reuters), 26 (Reuters),
29 (Ben Radford), 42–43 (Ben Radford); Getty Images
8 (Hulton Archive), 9 (AFP), 13 (Aurora), 15, 22 (AFP),
25, 27, 28 (AFP), 38 (AFP); Panos front cover (Mikkel
Ostergaard), 1 (Peter Barker), 10 (Peter Barker), 18
(Giacomo Pirozzi), 24 (Karen Robinson), 30 (GMB
Akash), 36 (Mark Henley), 41 (GMB Akash);
Photolibrary.com 6 (F1), 14 (Digital Vision); Reuters 33
(Andrea Comas), 39 (Parth Sanyal); Rugmark 35, 45;
Still Pictures 20 (Charlotte Thege/Das Fotoarchiv), 23
(Frans Lemmens); Topfoto.co.uk 37 (Ullstein Bild).

Cover picture: Children working as day laborers carry
vegetables to market in Sindhuwa, Nepal.

9 8 7 6 5 4 3 2 1

CONTENTS

WHAT IS CHILD LABOR?

A weekend job for extra pocket money might be fun but what about working in a dangerous factory, heaving rocks for hours without resting, or digging in trash for scraps to sell? Millions of children have to work like this every day.

Underage Workers

Child labor involves very young people in full-time, often dangerous, work. It is thought to affect one in six children around the world. Areas of work include farms, factories, building sites, dumps, and mines. Ten-year-old Zareen is a garbage picker in Afghanistan:

❝ I scavenge the garbage dump for things to sell. I have scars on my feet and arms from glass and sharp metal and my legs are covered in rashes. Sometimes, I choke on the fumes from chemicals. But I have to work there all day as I get paid almost nothing, just enough food to survive. ❞

Every day, this young boy collects waste from a large trash dump in Manila, Philippines. The work is tiring, unpleasant, and dangerous.

Number of full-time child laborers aged 5–17: 218 million

Number of these under the age of 14: 166 million

International Labor Organization (ILO), 2006

Protecting Children

More than 190 countries have agreed to protect children by signing the United Nations Convention on the Rights of the Child. Part of the agreement sets down rules against harmful work. This includes:

> **" The right of the child to be protected from economic exploitation and from performing any work that is likely to be hazardous or to interfere with the child's education, or to be harmful to the child's health or physical, mental, spiritual, moral, or social development. "**

Pie chart:
- Hazardous work, aged 5–11 (40 million)
- Hazardous work, aged 12–14 (34 million)
- Hazardous work, aged 15–17 (52 million)
- Other child labor, aged 5–17 (92 million)

As this pie chart shows, large numbers of children as young as five years old are involved in hazardous work—one of the worst forms of child labor.
ILO, Global Child Labor Trends, 2006

For the millions involved in child labor, these rights are brutally ignored.

HAZARDOUS WORK

Hazardous work includes work:

- Underground, underwater, at dangerous heights, or in confined spaces
- With dangerous machinery, equipment, and tools or heavy loads
- In an unhealthy environment or exposing children to abuse
- Under very difficult conditions such as long hours or during the night

ILO Recommendation No. 190 on the Worst Forms of Child Labor

IS CHILD LABOR A NEW ISSUE?

Articles and news about child labor appear throughout the media today. But has it always been a major issue?

A Long History

Children have worked for thousands of years on farms or as servants. During the Industrial Revolution in the eighteenth and nineteenth centuries, many large factories grew and had thousands of children working long hours in terrible conditions. John was just six when he was forced to work in a clothing mill in Derbyshire, England, in the 1840s:

❝ Our regular time was from five in the morning till nine or ten at night; and on Saturday till eleven and then we were sent to clean the machinery on the Sunday. No time was allowed for breakfast and no sitting for dinner . . . ❞

In this U.S. factory in the 1890s, young children spun thread for clothing. Adults supervised their work and would punish them for even the smallest error.

Children from Hyderabad, India, put on masks to mark World Day Against Child Labor on June 12, 2008. This event first appeared in the calendar in 2002.

Taking Notice

The earliest laws to reduce child labor appeared in the nineteenth century, but most efforts are much more recent. In the last 30 to 40 years, many charities and groups have started campaigning about the issue. Billy, a high-school student from California, gives his reasons for this new awareness:

❝ The Internet and TV let Americans and others in rich countries know so much more about conditions all over the world now. What we see is shocking. Maybe that's forced more people into action and has made child labor become a world issue. ❞

"The words 'child labor' elicit grim, dark images of nineteenth-century sweatshops and coal mines. But child labor remains stubbornly alive throughout much of the world . . . The human cost is immense: a childhood of hard labor often leaves children gaunt and crippled, sickly and uneducated."

NY Times journalist, Steven Greenhouse, *Encarta 1997 Yearbook*

IS CHILD LABOR WORSE IN TOWNS OR IN THE COUNTRY?

Children work all over the world in towns and cities and in the country. The work they do varies enormously, but is one area worse than the other?

Farmed Out

Agriculture is the biggest employer of underage workers. More than 150 million children work on farms, often doing backbreaking, exhausting jobs. In isolated rural villages, away from police and charities, abuse can take place unseen. Raki, who works as a jasmine flower picker in Egypt, is just nine years old:

" We have to work through the night for eight or nine hours to pick the flowers when their scent is strongest. Mosquitoes are everywhere. You always get bitten. I get paid 3 Egyptian pounds [54 cents] a day if I work hard. If I don't pick enough or feel ill or stop, I get paid less and whipped with a cane. "

Two very young children plant rice in a flooded field in Nepal. Child farmers may work 10–12 hours a day in planting or harvesting seasons.

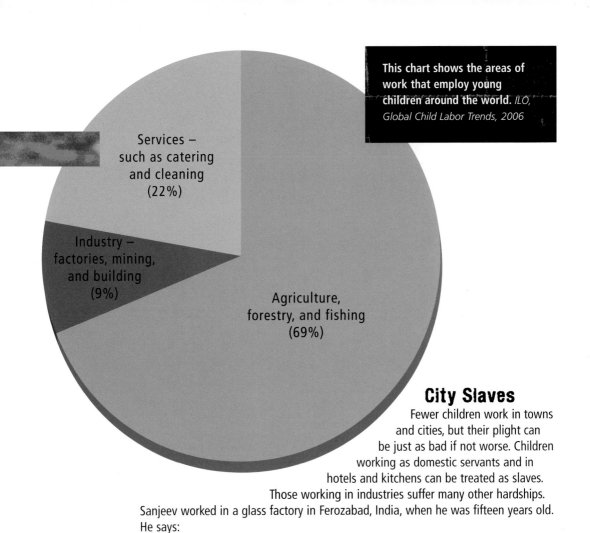

This chart shows the areas of work that employ young children around the world. *ILO, Global Child Labor Trends, 2006*

Services – such as catering and cleaning (22%)

Industry – factories, mining, and building (9%)

Agriculture, forestry, and fishing (69%)

City Slaves

Fewer children work in towns and cities, but their plight can be just as bad if not worse. Children working as domestic servants and in hotels and kitchens can be treated as slaves. Those working in industries suffer many other hardships. Sanjeev worked in a glass factory in Ferozabad, India, when he was fifteen years old. He says:

❝ Seven nights a week, we had to place glassware [like bowls, glasses, and bangles] inside a furnace without gloves or helmets. Of course, we got burned all the time and hit or starved if we cried. But the biggest danger turned out to be the coal dust and fumes you breathed in. Two years since I stopped working there, I still have trouble breathing. ❞

"For children working as domestic laborers, the hazards are sometimes not that obvious. Here, it can be the psychological hazards, like isolation, abuse, exploitation, that make this form dangerous."
World Health Organization, 2008

IS CHILD LABOR A PROBLEM IN WEALTHY COUNTRIES?

The vast majority of the world's child laborers are found in poorer, developing countries, mainly in Africa, Asia, and South and Central America. But does the problem exist in the developed world, too?

Protected By Law

Mikael is a young teen living in the Netherlands, one of the countries in the European Union (EU). He doesn't believe that there is much of a problem in his country, or in the EU as a whole:

" We have strong laws here and in the EU to stop child labor and welfare to help the poorest. No one has to work just to eat. I don't think it's much of a problem here, not compared to Africa with 50 million children working. "

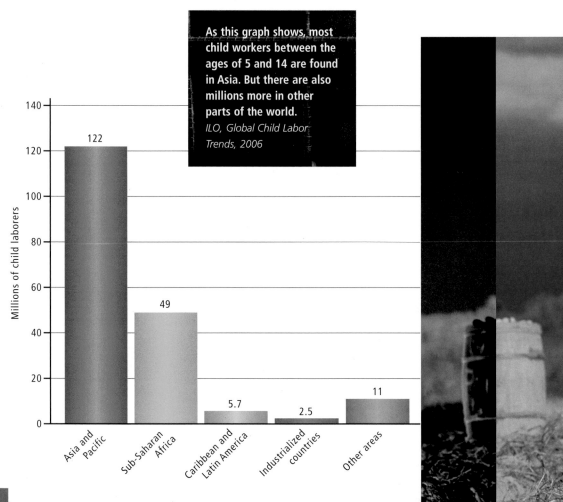

As this graph shows, most child workers between the ages of 5 and 14 are found in Asia. But there are also millions more in other parts of the world.
ILO, Global Child Labor Trends, 2006

Millions of child laborers

- Asia and Pacific: 122
- Sub-Saharan Africa: 49
- Caribbean and Latin America: 5.7
- Industrialized countries: 2.5
- Other areas: 11

Secret Struggle

For many, the issue of child labor is still not taken seriously enough. Illegal child labor does occur in wealthier nations, although it is often kept secret. The United States, for example, has an estimated 250,000 unlawful child laborers. Mani, who first worked on a farm in Arizona at age 12, was one of them:

❝ I worked in fields that had just been sprayed with chemicals that stung your eyes and made you choke. Sometimes, you passed out from the heat. There was very little drinking water and the older children or adults used to steal it from us younger kids. ❞

"Federal laws permit a child aged 13 to work in 100-degree heat in a strawberry field, but do not permit that child to work in an air-conditioned office. Under the Fair Labor Standards Act (FLSA) the legal age to perform most farm work is only 12 if a parent accompanies the working child."
Child Labor Coalition, 2007

A boy carries potatoes that he has harvested in a field in Maine. Some child farm laborers in wealthy countries work in tough conditions.

CAN'T WORK BE ENJOYABLE?

Much of the debate on child labor concentrates on the harm that work can do to children. Yet can't children's work be fun?

Millions of children volunteer to wash their parents' cars for extra pocket money. Doing jobs like this can help them learn about the value of money.

A Happy Experience

In many countries, children whose families aren't poor still choose to work part time. Some do so to earn cash for little extras, such as CDs or computer games. Others want to learn a skill or gain experience of a subject or hobby they enjoy. Annika, a Danish 12-year-old, works weekends at a riding stable:

❝ My family and I live in an apartment outside Copenhagen so we could never have a horse. But working here is the next best thing. I get to learn about horses and most days, get free rides. It's exciting and I get paid. ❞

"As long as adults don't misuse their power over children, the right kinds of work at the right age can be interesting, challenging, and good fun. Children are people too, and most people love the independence and pleasure of a job well done plus some cash into the bargain."

Brigid McConville, author of the book *Working Children*

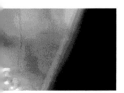

No Choice, No Fun

There is little joy for the millions of child workers who have to work all the time. Camel racing may sound fun, but not when you're taken from your home country of Bangladesh to Dubai, beaten, and forced to ride. This happened to Ahmed when he was five years old:

❝ I was scared . . . If I made a mistake I was beaten with a stick. When I said I wanted to go home I was told I never would. I didn't enjoy camel racing, I was really afraid. I fell off many times. When I won prizes several times, such as money and a car, the camel owner took everything. I never got anything, no money, nothing; my family also got nothing. ❞

Underage camel jockeys race in Kuwait. Many riders are poorly fed to keep their weight down and risk injury or death from falls and being trampled.

IS WORK WORSE FOR CHILDREN THAN ADULTS?

Work can be dull and unpleasant for anyone, but are there specific dangers that affect only children and not adults?

At Greater Risk

Children are incredibly vulnerable. Their bodies are still growing, and tough physical work can cripple them for life. Children are often powerless to fight back when they are bullied or threatened. They may not know their rights or are scared of reporting abuses to the police. Mai is a child factory worker in Indonesia:

❝ At night, I dream of the boy who ran away to the police. We never saw him again and the supervisor said he had been killed to teach us all a lesson. It is just easier to do what they tell us, even if it hurts. If you refuse, they will hurt you a lot more. ❞

Exhausted child workers in Colombia sleep crammed together in a small, dirty room. Children like this are easy targets for attack.

"Young workers not only face dangerous working conditions. They face long-term physical, intellectual, and emotional stress. They face an adulthood of unemployment and illiteracy."

Kofi Annan, former UN Secretary-General

More Resilient

A few people believe that children, unlike adults, have time on their side to recover from harsh experiences. They say that children are more adaptable and able to bounce back from problems. This landowner in Costa Rica thinks that children benefit from working for him:

❝ Children are quicker and more nimble than adults or machines. They are quicker to learn and easier to control. Many are idle or unruly when they come to me. They learn a sense of responsibility here. They develop character. Life is tough and by toughening them up, I give them the chance to survive when they get older. ❞

In demand for their small fingers and low wages, these children embroider carpets in the Pakistani city of Multan. Their shifts often last for ten hours or more.

LOST CHILDHOODS

- At least 22,000 children die each year in work-related accidents.

- The poisonous effects of pesticide chemicals sprayed on crops can be three times more dangerous to children than adults.

ILO, Environmental Protection Agency (EPA), UNICEF

SHOULDN'T CHILDREN BE IN SCHOOL?

A 2006 report indicated that approximately 115 million of the world's children are not going to school. Shouldn't all children be in school and not at work?

A Basic Human Right

Many people feel that all children should receive schooling as a basic human right. They say that education is the very best way for children to improve their future lives. Hongjiao is a Chinese boy from a poor family. He has benefited from a Save the Children program that pays much of the cost of his schooling:

" The teachers are very kind. They buy exercise books for us when we can't afford them . . . I like all the subjects— Chinese, mathematics and science. I'd like to go on to middle school because I don't want to have a hard life. "

Children study in a school in Malawi, funded by the charity UNICEF. Without the funding, they would be unlikely to get a proper education.

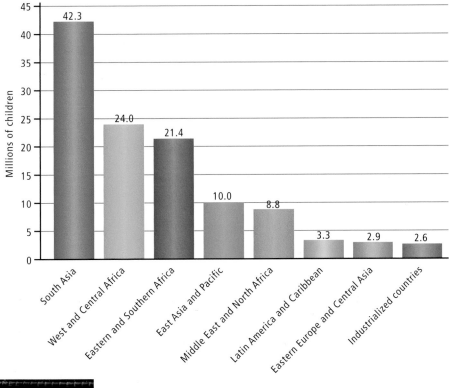

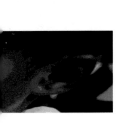

This graph shows how more than 115 million children worldwide are deprived of a school education. Most are in Africa and Asia.
UNESCO Institute of Statistics, 2006

"Children are the future. Save the Children are aware that adults who have gone to school for four years will earn twice as much as adults with no education."

Mimi Jakobsen, Save the Children Denmark, 2007

"Everyone has the right to education. Education shall be free, at least in the elementary stages. Elementary education shall be compulsory."

The Universal Declaration of Human Rights, 1948

Not an Option

Not all children are lucky enough to have their education paid for. Sometimes there are no schools within reach, or the fees are too high for desperately poor families to afford. Nine-year-old Tena, living in Congo, doubts he could go to school even if there was one nearby:

My biggest dream is to go to school, to learn how to read and write and to play with other children. The nearest school is a day's walk away. But, anyway, my mother is sick [from HIV/AIDS] and I have to work every day so that we can eat and afford medicine.

CAN CHILD LABOR HELP POOR FAMILIES?

Almost one-sixth of the world population lives in extreme poverty. Each day can be a struggle to obtain enough food, water, and other essentials to live. Can child labor help?

Kenyan children pick tea leaves from their family's plot. Without child workers, many small farms and businesses would struggle or fail.

Work or Starve

In many desperately poor regions of the world, even the smallest wage from a working child can mean the difference between life and death. In Sierra Leone, West Africa, 78 percent of all children work. One of them is eight-year-old Jebediah:

" If I don't work, no one is going to come and save our family. There is no help. Just men who pay me 400 leones [about 8 cents] to collect garbage. My money is not much, but all our family works. Who else is going to feed us? "

An Endless Cycle

Many people believe that working full time just keeps children in a cycle of poverty. Missing out on an education means they are unlikely to get a good job or earn sufficient money as an adult. Instead they can become, like 18-year-old Tamra in Tajikistan, trapped in extreme poverty and misery:

" No schooling and no future for me and now I have a baby, things are worse. I am forced to work selling my body to filthy men just to feed my baby. I want him to have a better future than I face. "

This family of carpet weavers in Kabul, Afghanistan, is so poor that each one of them has to work to survive.

"Because child labor usually keeps children out of school, in poor health, and exposes them to psychological and physical abuse, it reinforces this poverty by keeping yet another generation from fulfilling its potential."

Sheldon Yett, UNICEF Representative in Armenia, 2005

ISN'T IT THE PARENTS' FAULT?

Parents have a vital duty to look after their children and protect them from harm. Are they failing by sending their children to work?

Forced by Parents

Disturbingly large numbers of children are abused, abandoned, or forced into harsh work by their own parents. Around 8.4 million children, most in Nepal, India, and Pakistan, are sold into a form of slavery called bonded labor. This is often to pay off parents' debts, as happened to Ashmal in Pakistan:

" My father got into debt with his zamindar [landlord]. I think he gambled our money. I was taken to work making rugs to pay off the debt. I was locked up at night to stop me escaping. I was told it would take two years before I could go home. **"**

These Indian children were rescued from bonded labor in 2008. Some were as young as seven.

NO PARENTS

- Total number of orphans in Africa, Latin America, Asia, and the Caribbean: 143 million.

- One in eight of all children in southern Africa are orphans.

- Number of children orphaned by HIV/AIDS is expected to reach 20 million by 2010.

UNICEF, Global AIDS Alliance, 2007

"The children in the mining town of Uncia in the Department of Potosí [Bolivia] gaze at visitors with eyes and faces that look old beyond their years. They don't smile. They don't play. They sit slumped in their chairs, tired and listless."
ABA *Human Rights* Magazine, 2005

Replacing Parents

Many children are forced into work because their parents have died, making them orphans. Others have parents who are physically unable to work. For some families, sending a child to work is a tough decision but one that has to be made. José, age 11, is one of more than 6,000 children working in the metal mines of Potosí, Bolivia:

❝ With my father sick, there is no choice. My mother works on the surface but you get paid three times as much to work underground and I am small enough to crawl through the shafts to pull rock out. It is hard work for ten hours a day but I love my father and mother. ❞

A Bolivian child climbs up out of a deep tin mine in Potosí. Thousands of child miners around the world suffer from muscle damage, broken bones, and painful breathing problems.

WHY ARE CHILDREN VICTIMS OF TRAFFICKING?

Human trafficking involves deceiving or forcing someone to move from their home to another region or country. There, they are exploited or made to work. Why are children trafficked?

This Lithuanian girl was trafficked to the UK, where she was forced to work as a prostitute. She finally escaped but needed support to recover from her experience.

Sex Trafficking

The International Labor Organization estimates that 1.2 million children are trafficked each year. Many of these are young boys or girls like Natalia, who are taken to a new country and forced to work in the sex industry:

❝ I am 15 now, but when I was 12 I was stolen from my village in Lithuania and put on a ship. I was kept in a room for months in Britain and told to go with the men who arrived. If I refused I was hit on my body and legs, never my face. I learned to do what they say. It was less painful. ❞

"Child victims of trafficking often experience mental and/or physical abuse by their traffickers. The experience of being trafficked can lead to depression and suicide. Furthermore, the stigma faced by victims and the risk of re-trafficking can make it difficult for children to be reunited with their families or communities."

UNICEF UK, 2008

A Life of Crime

Being removed from their family, isolated, and vulnerable in a new country can make children willing to do anything that traffickers ask. This may include performing crimes, as 13-year-old Choy found out when he was trafficked from Cambodia:

❝ I was promised training to become a mechanic. I was excited but when I arrived, I was forced to steal and work in a gang. They threatened to kill me if I didn't steal enough. I couldn't speak the language and had no one to turn to. We beat people up, stole, broke into homes. The police catching me was a relief. ❞

Many trafficked children are found and rescued. However, the abuse they have suffered can make it hard for them to fit back in with their families and communities at home.

A group of criminals stand on trial for trafficking 38 children in China in 2005. The shortest prison sentence that any of the men received was six years.

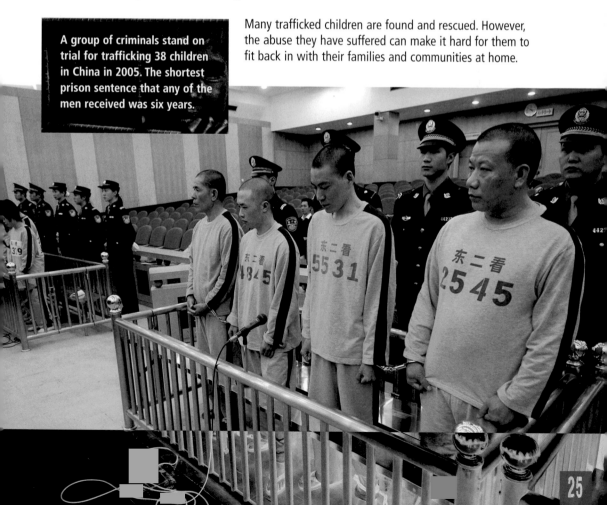

SHOULD CHILD SOLDIERS EVER EXIST?

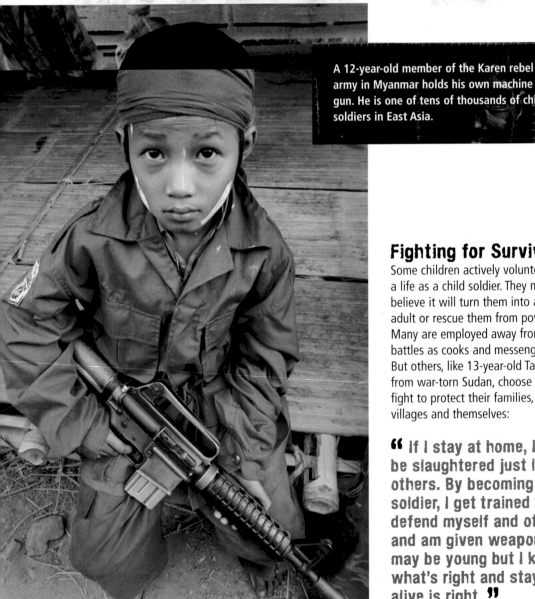

One of the most brutal forms of child labor is children as young as eight becoming soldiers. Child soldiers exist all over the world, from Indonesia to Colombia, Chad to Uzbekistan. Is there ever an excuse for children being forced to fight?

A 12-year-old member of the Karen rebel army in Myanmar holds his own machine gun. He is one of tens of thousands of child soldiers in East Asia.

Fighting for Survival

Some children actively volunteer for a life as a child soldier. They may believe it will turn them into an adult or rescue them from poverty. Many are employed away from battles as cooks and messengers. But others, like 13-year-old Tariq from war-torn Sudan, choose to fight to protect their families, villages and themselves:

❝ If I stay at home, I will be slaughtered just like others. By becoming a soldier, I get trained to defend myself and others and am given weapons. I may be young but I know what's right and staying alive is right. ❞

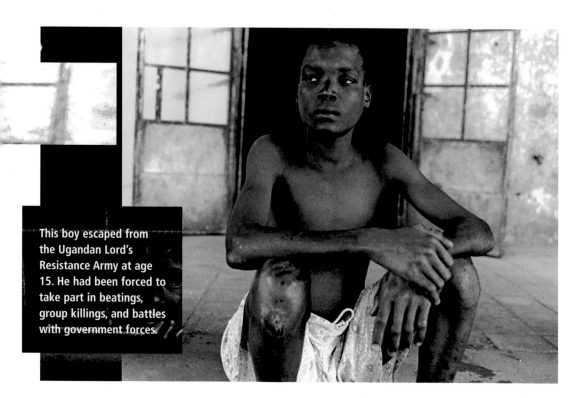

This boy escaped from the Ugandan Lord's Resistance Army at age 15. He had been forced to take part in beatings, group killings, and battles with government forces.

Brutal and Scarring

The vast majority of child soldiers are recruited by adults using threats or brute force. Many are made to fight or witness terrible acts of violence that will scar them forever. "M" recounts the terrible experiences he went through at age 12 when recruited by the Lord's Resistance Army (LRA) in Uganda:

❝ Early on when my brothers and I were captured, the LRA explained to us that all five brothers couldn't serve in the LRA because we would not perform well. So they tied up my younger brothers and invited us to watch. Then they beat them with sticks until two of them died. They told us it would give us strength to fight. My youngest brother was nine years old. ❞

"It is immoral that adults should want children to fight their wars for them . . . There is simply no excuse, no acceptable argument for arming children."
Nobel Peace Prize winner
Archbishop Desmond Tutu

AFRICA AND BEYOND

Total number of child soldiers:	Over 300,000
Number of child soldiers in Africa:	Over 170,000
Number of countries with child soldiers used in conflicts:	35–45

Note: These are estimates and thought to be less than the total numbers.
UN and Africa in Action

SHOULD THERE BE ONE AGE FOR ADULTHOOD?

Some countries have a minimum age above which most children are allowed to work. Should there be a universal set age for children to become adults who can therefore work, vote, and do other adult things?

One Age for All

Minimum ages for work, voting in elections, and other adult tasks often vary. In the UK, people can leave school and start work at 16, but have to be 17 to drive and 18 to vote. Is this confusing? Jenna, an American teen, thinks that a global set age could make matters simpler:

" One age to turn from child to adult would be cool. It would make checking out whether child workers were being used much easier to spot by the authorities. Adults exploiting children wouldn't be able to say they were confused by the laws. "

Recommended minimum ages have not ended child labor in many countries. This four-year-old boy works as a blacksmith in a factory in Baghdad, Iraq.

Schoolchildren in Ghana enjoy a game of soccer. Would a single age limit allow more children to enjoy childhood before becoming adults?

RECOMMENDATIONS FOR MINIMUM AGE

Hazardous work	18
Hazardous work under strict safety conditions	16
Basic minimum age (for full-time work)	15
Basic minimum age (possible exceptions for developing nations)	14
Light work (which doesn't threaten their health or schooling)	13–15
Light work (possible exceptions for developing nations)	12–14

ILO Convention No. 138, 1973

Who Decides?

Who should establish a minimum "adult" age? The International Labor Organization has a series of guidelines (see above). Yet some cultures in Africa and Asia think of children reaching adulthood much earlier. Ousmane from Bamakó, Mali, feels that wealthy countries do not have the right to set an age for all:

" Rich countries have exploited Mali for centuries so why should we let them decide our fates? In my country, children become adults earlier. If you make 45 here, you are in old age. Most people die before they are 60, so we need to be counted as adults as early as possible. "

SHOULDN'T WE BAN SWEATSHOPS?

A large number of child laborers work in sweatshops. These are factories, often making apparel (clothing and footwear), where conditions vary from poor to atrocious and the pay is extremely low.

Degrading and Violent

Many people feel that sweatshops should be banned because they are so degrading. In 2007, a UK newspaper uncovered terrible conditions in an Indian sweatshop making clothing for a leading manufacturer. Jivaj, age 12, was one of the children there:

❝ Our hours are hard and violence is used against us if we don't work hard enough. This is a big order for abroad, they keep telling us that. Last week, we spent four days working from dawn until about one o'clock in the morning the following day. I was so tired I felt sick. If any of us cried we were hit with a rubber pipe. Some of the boys had oily cloths stuffed in their mouths as punishment. ❞

The owner of a clothing workshop in Dhaka, Bangladesh, threatens to beat a child employee. The boy is paid just one dollar for a ten-hour working day.

Large factories like this one in Ho Chi Minh City, Vietnam, provide jobs for thousands of workers, some of whom are children.

Best of the Worst

Supporters argue that sweatshops play a vital role in helping poorer countries to develop their industries. Some believe that closing sweatshops will result in children moving into even worse-paid, more horrific jobs such as mining and prostitution. It's a fear shared by Songai, a 14-year-old sweatshop worker in Indonesia:

❝ I get paid more here than working on a farm or hustling on streets. I don't want to do those things. Why not make laws that we can drink water and go to the toilet when we want to? Improve our pay and our conditions, but don't close our workplace down. ❞

"[Having more sweatshops] gives the workers more employers to choose from, raises productivity and wages, and eventually improves working conditions. This is the same process of economic development the U.S. went through, and it is ultimately the way Third World workers will raise their standard of living."
Economists Benjamin Powell and David Skarbek, writing in the *Christian Science Monitor*, 2005

ARE MULTINATIONALS TO BLAME?

Multinationals, or transnationals, are big businesses that operate in a number of countries. Many rely on raw materials, parts, or finished goods that are supplied by poorer countries where child labor is common.

Keeping Child Labor Secret

Critics of multinationals state that all they care about are low costs and big profits. Big businesses push local suppliers to produce as cheaply as possible, even if that involves child labor. Huong is 14 and works in a Vietnamese factory making footwear sold by major brands:

" Every few months, inspectors visit from the big company. They're not blind. They must smell the fumes, see the filth that we work in. But the first inspection was over two years ago and nothing has changed. We're still forced to glue 100 pairs of shoes per hour or we don't get paid. "

Young workers shape shoe moldings in a Vietnamese factory. This is one of several factories in Vietnam that produce footwear for the sportswear multinational, Nike.

"Apparel industry wages are low by U.S. standards, but they compare favorably with the average standard of living in these countries. Apparel workers in the Dominican Republic, Haiti, Honduras, and Nicaragua earn three to seven times the national average."

Benjamin Powell and David Skarbek, *Sweatshops and Third World Living Standards*, 2006

"While 96 percent of U.S. business leaders think their company's corporate social responsibility behavior will greatly impact the nation's economic future, more than 40 percent still don't have any policy in place to guide their company's actions."

American Society for Quality, 2006

A girl poses as a faceless worker during a protest against large companies making clothing for the 2004 Olympics. Some of the companies exploited their workers.

Sound Sourcing

Most multinationals say they try to practice sound sourcing. This means regularly inspecting their suppliers' facilities and checking for an absence of child labor. Kurt worked for a multinational that found children were involved in its supply chain:

❝ We were strongly against child labor. It wasn't even our suppliers, but a company who supplied them. We cancelled our suppliers' contracts straight away and removed the products from our shelves. Still, the media blamed us. ❞

ARE CONSUMERS TO BLAME?

Consumers in developed countries may be wealthy, but they still demand low prices. Companies may end up using child labor just to keep their costs down. Is this the consumers' fault?

This chart shows the results of a survey that asked 980 Australian shoppers to check what was very important to them when buying clothes.
Choice, Consumer Awareness Survey, 2008

Price Sensitive

Polls show that consumers are often more concerned about prices or animal welfare than whether child labor was involved. Lars, age 15, is from Odense, Denmark. He worries that people won't demand or pay extra for guaranteed child labor-free items:

❝ It's just a few euros more on everyone's bill to make sure child labor isn't involved in what you buy. Companies would quickly act if their goods made with child labor stayed on the shelves. But people choose to ignore and stay ignorant. They don't care and are greedy and want as much as possible. ❞

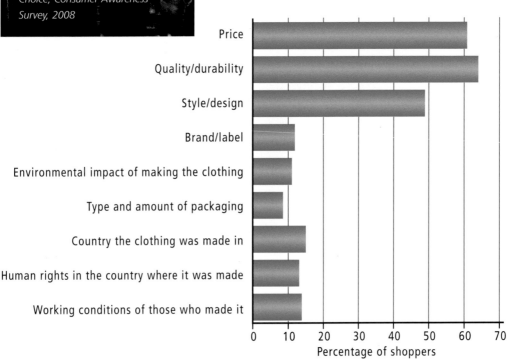

	Percentage of shoppers
Price	~61
Quality/durability	~64
Style/design	~49
Brand/label	~11
Environmental impact of making the clothing	~10
Type and amount of packaging	~8
Country the clothing was made in	~15
Human rights in the country where it was made	~12
Working conditions of those who made it	~13

A boy studies at a school in Nepal run by the charitable organization Rugmark. Carpets featuring the Rugmark logo (foreground right) are guaranteed to have been made without child labor.

Confusion and Secrecy

Should consumers be given more information? Only some goods are branded fair or ethical trade. Some companies claim that they don't know whether child labor is involved in their products—or they keep it secret. Ibrahim, who works in the chocolate trade in West Africa, believes that companies should be more truthful:

❝ Cocoa [which is used to make chocolate] prices are terrible, very low. Many farmers here use children for 12 hours each shift just to survive. Who sets the prices? The big companies. But do they tell their customers what they are doing? No, they tell lies. ❞

"The public has a major role to play in the fight against child labor. They need to learn more about who makes the products they buy, and support organizations with programs to stop child labor."

Bhuwan Ribhu, campaigner for the Global March Against Child Labor

CAN LAWS AND AGREEMENTS HELP?

Governments have passed laws against child labor and signed major international agreements, like the UN Convention on the Rights of the Child. So how is it that child labor continues?

Students at a college in Mexico City celebrate their graduation. Mexico has taken steps to reduce child labor, but many thousands of Mexican children still work full time.

Making Progress

Laws and agreements, when backed with money and support, can make a difference. Between 2000 and 2004, the number of child workers in Latin America and the Caribbean dropped by two-thirds. In Brazil, new laws were combined with payments to families to keep children in school. These changes saw a 61 percent drop in 5- to 9-year-old child workers within 12 years. Seba is one of those who has benefited:

❝ I don't understand politics and laws but I think they have done good here. I have read about history in other countries. The USA once had millions of child workers like me but laws mean it now has very few. I was working as a servant at age nine, now I am studying to go to technical college. ❞

A young Indian girl sells spices in the streets of Kolkata, despite a law that bans children from this type of work.

Needing Back-Up

Creating new laws and making them work can be two different things. In 2006, a new law in India banned children under the age of 14 from being domestic workers or food stall sellers. Rita, director of a child rights organization in Delhi, believes this is not enough on its own:

❝ The ban has come without any prior planning for restoration and rehabilitation of children who will be affected. It is ridiculous to think that announcing a ban alone will end child abuse and exploitation. ❞

"The only way for children to have the childhood that labor robs from them is for governments, local and national, to strictly enforce laws regulating child labor and punish those who forego them."

Dr A. K. Shiva Kumar, development economist and consultant to the United Nations

CAN INDIVIDUALS MAKE A DIFFERENCE?

As individuals, we can learn more about child labor, pick what we buy carefully, donate to charities, and join anti-child-labor groups. Can this type of action really help?

Too Big a Task

Some people believe that child labor is necessary for starving families to survive. Others feel that the problem is impossible to solve because it is so wrapped up in major issues such as world poverty. Zhou from Singapore is one of those who feels that there is little she can do:

❝ How can one person make a difference against the economies of the world? While poverty exists, children will always be forced to work. It is too big an issue for any one person to solve and if it can't be solved, why bother wasting your time trying to help? ❞

Prateep Ungsongtham Hata was once a child laborer in Thailand. She has since won awards for her many years of fighting to improve the lives of child workers.

Former Indian child workers make their beds in a Free the Children home. The organization has also built more than 500 schools to give children a chance of a better life.

Making a Difference

Canadian Craig Kielburger was just 12 years old when he founded the charity Free the Children in 1995. His organization has since collected thousands of dollars to buy children out of bondage and set up learning centers in India. He feels that individuals can make a real difference and that adults should be doing a lot, lot more:

❝ I simply do not believe that the adults of the world can put a man on the moon or invent the atom bomb and cannot free the children of the world. I won't give up until the exploitation of all children has ended and all children have their rights. ❞

"The elimination of [all] child labor is a long-term objective. However, in the meanwhile, we cannot allow that children are injured or harmed at work in their struggle for survival, especially when we have the knowledge and means to prevent this."

World Health Organization, 2008

WHAT DOES THE FUTURE HOLD?

Child labor remains a powerful, disturbing, and complicated world issue. Can it be properly addressed, or will it always exist?

Hope for the Future

Statistics show that between 2000 and 2004, the number of child laborers worldwide dropped by 38 million. Campaigns, news reports, extra money, and new laws have all helped. In addition, wealthy countries have cancelled some of the debts owed by the poorest countries. In Tanzania, more than 1.6 million extra children have joined schools since 2002—including 14-year-old Habib:

" School is hard but fun. After years of working, I have much catching up to do. I am thankful to no longer be working crushing stones in quarries. My breathing and health are better and my nightmares have stopped. "

This graph shows reductions in child labor between the years 2002 and 2004. *Statistical Information and Monitoring Program on Child Labor (SIMPOC), 2006*

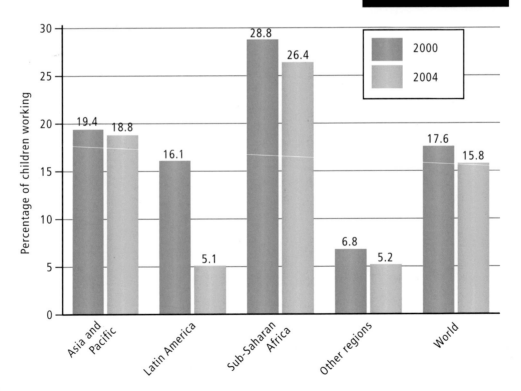

Still So Much to Be Done

While successes have occurred, the stark fact remains that many millions of children are still having their childhoods stolen. They continue to work in tough and sometimes terrifying conditions, like Gilberto, an 11-year-old in Haiti:

❝ I was a restavek (a child domestic servant) but then got kicked out. I now work in an old food factory. The machinery breaks down and we have to crawl in between the blades to fix it. Three boys, including my best friend, Pani, were killed when the machine started up again. It was horrible. ❞

It may be too late to help Gilberto's friends, and many others who have been killed or scarred physically or emotionally by child labor. But it is not too late for many millions more.

A child stares out from a silver cooking pot factory in Bangladesh. In this country, over 17 percent of children aged 5–15 still work in largely unacceptable conditions.

1780s onward The Industrial Revolution, first in Britain, then in other parts of Europe and the United States, sees giant factories often employing children as young as six.

1802 The 1802 Factory Act is one of the earliest laws against child labor. However, it only makes it illegal for children to work more than 12 hours a day.

1833 The 1833 Factory Act declares that British children must attend school for two hours per day.

1836 Massachusetts is the first U.S. state to make a law requiring children under 15 to attend school for at least three months per year.

1839 Prussia (a European state until 1947) passes laws on child labor, making night shifts and Sunday working illegal.

1870 The U.S. Census reports that 750,000 children, aged 10–15, are working full time.

1873 Denmark passes its first child labor law, making it illegal to employ children under the age of 10.

1904 The National Child Labor Committee is formed in the United States to challenge sweatshops and child labor.

1911 A fire at the Triangle Shirtwaist Factory kills 148 young clothing workers in New York.

1919 The International Labor Organization (ILO) is formed.

1919 The Save the Children organization is founded by two British sisters, Eglantyne Jebb and Dorothy Buxton.

1929 The Wall Street crash sees economies collapse and sets off the Great Depression, creating much poverty throughout the world in the 1930s.

1933 The first law of its kind in India makes selling a child to pay debts illegal.

1938 The first national minimum age and maximum hours for child workers are set in the United States with the passing of the Fair Labor Standards Act.

1973   The Minimum Age Convention (No. 138) is produced by the ILO.

1988   The first Fairtrade label is launched, selling coffee in the Netherlands.

1989   The United Nations Convention on the Rights of the Child is held.

1990   The World Summit for Children is held in New York and is attended by the heads of 71 countries.

1992   The ILO establishes the International Program on the Elimination of Child Labor (IPEC).

1996   ILO statistics show that 41 percent of all children in Africa are child laborers.

1998   Soccer balls used and sold for the FIFA World Cup are found to have been made using child labor.

1999   The world population passes 6 billion for the first time. Approximately one in three are children.

2000   Statistics show that there are some 246 million child laborers around the world.

2002   The ILO produces its first global report on child labor. The first World Day Against Child Labor is held.

2005   The U.S. chain Wal-Mart is fined $135,000 for allowing teenage workers to operate hazardous equipment.

2006   The ILO's second global report on child labor says that child labor is declining worldwide.

2007   Gap removes some children's clothing from sale after campaigns reveal that child workers were involved in its production.

2008   World Day Against Child Labor focuses on the campaign for all children to receive an education.

GLOSSARY

abuse To treat a person in a cruel or violent way, including sexually.

bonded labor When people, often children, are forced to work for others—sometimes for a period of years—to pay off a debt.

consumer Someone who buys or uses something.

developed nations Wealthy nations like the United States, United Kingdom and most of western Europe, with large industries and relatively high average income per member of population.

developing nations Nations seeking to build their industries and wealth, who tend to be poorer and contain many poor people.

domestic service Work performed by people in a household as servants.

economic of or relating to the system of making, distributing, and using money or wealth.

European Union (EU) A political and economic grouping of more than 20 European nations who act as one large trading zone. Many share a common currency called the Euro.

exploitation Forcing people to work extremely hard and paying them very little or nothing to make big profits.

human rights The basic rights of all people, such as the right to free speech, shelter, and food.

illegal Against the laws of a country or local area.

multinational A large company with offices and/or factories in several countries.

pesticides Chemicals sprayed on farmland or crops to kill insects, which can sometimes be harmful to people.

prostitution The industry or action of offering sex in return for money.

supply chain The network of companies who are involved in making a product, including those who supply its parts or raw materials and those who transport, store, and sell it.

sweatshop A shop or factory in which employees work for long hours for low wages in dangerous and unpleasant conditions.

trafficking Removing people by force from their community, imprisoning them, and often selling them abroad or in another part of the country.

UNICEF Part of the United Nations, responsible for children's health, education, and well-being.

United Nations (UN) An international organization with more than 190 member countries, which was formed in 1945 to promote world peace, good health, and economic development.

vulnerable Especially at risk.

RESOURCES

Books

Child Labor and Sweatshops by Ann Manheimer (Greenhaven Press, 2006)

Children at Work: Child Labor Practices in Africa by Anne Kielland and Maurizia Tovo (Lynne Rienner Publishers, 2006)

Elizabeth Bloomer: Child Labor Activist by Jennifer Reed (KidHaven Press, 2006)

Free the Children: A Young Man's Personal Crusade Against Child Labor by Craig Kielburger and Kevin Major (HarperCollins, 1998)

Web Sites

http://www.savethechildren.net/alliance/index.html
The official web site of the Save the Children charity, which campaigns to improve children's lives all over the world. This site contains links to national sites for Canada, the United States, the United Kingdom and many others.

http://www.freethechildren.com
The official web site of Free the Children, a network of children that help children through education. Craig Kielburger, who was 12 years old at the time, founded the network in 1995. The organization fights child labor in 45 different countries.

http://www.childlaborphotoproject.org
Child Labor and the Global Village: Photography for Social Change is a team of 11 photographers who will be photographing child workers around the globe. The web site showcases their photography and provides links to other web sites about child labor.

http://www.continuetolearn.uiowa.edu/laborctr/child_labor/links.html
An excellent collection of links to child labor web sites.

http://www.unicef.org.uk/publications/pdf/ECECHILD2_A4.pdf
A downloadable free guide to child labor issues from UNICEF.

http://www.child-soldiers.org/home
The web site of the Coalition to Stop the Use of Child Soldiers, which contains reports and the experiences of child soldiers in their own words.

INDEX